Stumblin' Up the High Road

Sian Lexmond

BookLeaf
Publishing

India | USA | UK

Presentation by *BookLeaf Publishing*

Web: www.bookleafpub.com

E-mail: info@bookleafpub.com

ISBN: 9789357447171

First edition 2022

What is a beginning?

What is a beginning?
Why, it's a start of course!
And what is a start?
Err, well, it's.. the beginning

I'll be more precise shall I

What do you define as the start?
Is it the moment we make the initial action that
propels us forward? Or the moment we first put
pen to paper to plan? Or the moment the idea
first coalesces in our minds?
Why not go further back and make the
beginning the point
when our minds suddenly became capable of
thought?
And and and...

The starting step is always the hardest
Like the capital letter at the start of a sentence,
        it IS important.
But, what that step *looks like* is not.

However tiny the forward shuffle or
gargantuan the initial leap,
a start puts us on our path
and we simply have to follow.

Cut Flowers

"I'll never understand why people give
                                        dead
flowers"

"These are gorgeous when they bloom
                    but then they drop their
petals"

"Hey hey, they're alive to start with"
        "Yeah, they live just as long as my
patience"

"Why give someone something so nice
                            that just doesn't
last"

"They're pretty, yes,
                            but then they
die"

live fast die beautiful
Excuse me, they are simply living the dream

Trickster God?

I cannot tell you about the trickster god
For they give no answers
They stopped me in the street one night
They just wanted the banters

I was warned straightaway
Ne'er to ask a question
For this was a night of peace
Not an interrogation

I had many things to ask
Like were they more shadow or crow
But I tried to heed their words
And simply lamented the snow

That night, that stroll, I did enjoy
I found their quietness calming
I wondered what would happen when
The new day was sadly dawning

But I refused to think those thoughts
I wanted to stay in the moment
For when they became just memories
Regret wouldn't be my opponent

And yet, at last I could take no more
I had to know one thing
"Why me?" I asked. And they were
Gone, that silence was a sting.

I cannot tell you about the trickster god
For they give no answers
But if you meet me out one night
I may choose you for the banters

Accepting Lies

We live in a society
where we value honesty

If you were to lie to me
that would be a travesty

But in life's entirety
lies are an eventuality

It's that irresistibility
of life's imagined fantasticality

Yet truly escaping reality
is noted for its impossibility

So we attempt rejecting fictionality
to strive for authenticity

In all situations save one-
"I'll only nap for like 20 min"

Gosh, I miss my cat

I sit down to do work
All my books are still on the desk
and immediately accessible
(Gosh, I miss my cat)

I open my closet
My black clothes are sleek
and still, actually completely black
(Gosh, I miss my cat)

I make my bed
The bedsheet immediately lies flat
This is way too efficient
(Gosh, I miss my cat)

I am lying in bed
Sleeping past sunrise is no longer
an infrequent luxury
(Gosh, I miss my cat)

I am doing anything in life
Everything is easier, simpler, fluffless
but I carry this hole in my heart
(Gosh, I miss my cat)

The Infernal Debate

The day I saw it,
it shook my world.
Something so simple,
a solution so
elegant... How
had I not thought
of it before?
But now, now it is
seared into my
mind. Now & forever.

      It goes round in
circles. 'Zee' or 'zed'?
'Zed' or 'zee'? No need
to be agitated or angry.
Some say it should
be 'zee'
to rhyme
with the 'ABC's.
        Yes. Valid. Acceptable.
But now,
I put forth...
'zee' so I may
shorten
    disease to 'DZ'.

Meditation

...thispaperduethepresentationtomorrowrentisco
minguphowmanybrowniesdoineedfortheeventho
wmanyshoesarecomingofftheponieswilltherebee
noughtodecoratewhenareexamspathologywhatev
enisdysplasiashouldigeticedcoffeedoievenlikecof
feeomgihaven'twritteninmydiaryforawhilehowa
mifeelin

Enter in a working trot at A

A switch flips.
Peace. Focus.
Suddenly, I am aware of
        nothing,
but this bubble.
            Me and the horse.
        Two hearts.
One ride.
Months of training for these five
or six minutes. Of course I
cannot think of anything else.

Almost akin to slow motion,
each step is completed and
flows through to the next.

I have time to ponder each
movement, understand what
goes well or not, But I
file these away. A time will
come for analysis, for now I simply
Enjoy the Ride.

Turn down the centreline

Here it comes.
The rush, the onslaught.
These moments of
pure concentration
are heaven.
What would I ever do without...
I wouldn't survive if I didn't...
have a horse in my life.

It is true, this is my only Meditation

Halt at X. Salute.

it'soverweactuallymadeitthroughthewholetestthis
isawesomeohmythismaredeservesallthecarrotssh
ewassogoodmmmcarrotsohiwonderwhatthereisf
orlunchdoihavetimeforlunchohdamnthatpapertha
tpresentationthexams...

Questions

What is life? How is life? Why is life?

Ask a hundred different people
Get 102 different answers

Figure that one out eh?

But what more is there to say?

So many avenues for chancers,
Life could do with many a sequel.

So we just keep pushing through the strife

A Match

I used to think a conversation was like a tennis
match
Two players stand on a court,
Opposite and ready
It begins.

"Hello"
"How are you?"

The volley starts small
The ball leisurely making its way from side to
side
Soon, the players get more comfortable
        playing the game,
They move more easily
More enjoyably
Personal information whistling back and forth
Through the air

Suddenly the climax of the game
The first secret backhanded to the other side
Inner thoughts shared
        without fear of judgement
Is this.. real appreciation?

Are we suddenly true confidantes?

We each find a different part of this intrigue
        overwhelming
but we keep returning shots, keep trying
because we want to keep the ball afloat,
waltzing effortlessly through the air
as we keep the conversation stoked...

Sometimes I think a conversation
is like a tennis match
other times,
it is simply just like a match
And I would rather burn myself
than speak to you <3

Heart of Diamond

It is beauty like no other
When the light hits just right,
It is refracted all around
Beautiful patterns twining their way
      into the ether,
Shadows dance and play between
      pure beams,
Effervescent in the dazzling glory.

When her heart is surrounded
      by love,
It is beauty like no other.
She channels it through many facets
To light the lives of others,
Clearing darkness of doubt by
      playing,
dancing the shadows away.

And yet, it sits not right.
For without another body to
      feed off,
Her heart sits cold and empty.
No light and warmth can radiate from
      that which is without
It's own source of love.

The desperation with which she clings to
                        someone
              everyone
          anyone
else,
It is hard not to feel beaten and bruised
by that endless battering of her
most wondrous stone heart.

In these moments, I am glad I lack
A heart of diamond
           may be stunning to behold
But beware,
Those beauteous edges are sharp enough
to cut.

What is a journey?

I invite you on a journey.
A walk. Not on the wild side,
but on YOUR wild side.

Life gets so hectic
We get so lost in everything
I invite you to take a moment
and ponder the randomness of life

Can we hope to piece it all together
as a coherent journey?
Do our brains have that setting?

Yet,
part of the beauty is the variety and the questions
So on the path, any path, your path
Take a moment, take a breath, take a few
random steps
to mess about.
Every problem has its place
and we'll get there in time

What "there" is.. is up to you.
You assign your own meaning.
Life is what you make it.

kitty cuddles

she stalks in silence
muscles bunch, waiting to pounce
an ambush of love

All Alone

Alone?
   All
      on
         my
            own.
Is that a bad thing?
Not all the time.

But not if I choose.
Sometimes
      (but not all the time)
the space, the peace,
the quiet, the solitude,
the time inside my own
brain can be a blessing.
But
    only when I grant it.
When I need those moments
to get away, to allow me to be
more in the moment.
I couldn't go without.

And yet, force solitude on someone
and the story switches.

suddenly the once wondrous quiet
becomes oppressive
the peace turns to panic
"Don't leave me...
          What did I do...
                    I'm sorry..."

Our lives come down to
                    choices.
I choose to be alone sometimes
But never lonely.
I only hope you choose me too

Twilight

In A World
      Based Around Fact
There Are Few Spaces
    To Escape....

and yet, the twilight zone
      e x i s t s.
A space between wor lds.
A moment out of
        time.

It looks like just another building
but so many lives, so many stories
have filtered through.
Few places capture the true
zeitgeist of life.
But airports are bathed in the essence of it.

Voices in my Mind

You learn very quickly
that speaking very strictly,
you're never truly alone.

A consciousness may be meek,
but mine just learned to speak,
and recently, it won't shut up.

I ask myself "what reason?"
for surely these thoughts are treason.
Unfortunately they're just too much fun.

What would it be like to fly?
Will I have a legacy after I die?
Wait, what's the opposite of sushi?

So many questions, but never left hanging,
just to engage, this conversation is banging,
I could talk to me all night.

These voices in my mind,
are they poison, or are they prime-
ing me for more?
(I was told not to do that but I do what I want!)

Haiz will I ever know?

Potato Cactus

Few things
haunt me
as such.
But this,
two words
so simple
and yet
no ideas
came forth.
No story
formed itself
in the
confines of
my mind.
Such randomness,
it seems
perfect for
creativity abound.
But perhaps
that is
the issue,
there are
too many
options available.

How do
you pick
one?

Brightness

It is too much.
They are coming for me again.
The.. Colours..

Every morning I open my eyes
and they are there.
There is no escape
        why is there no escape?
Everyone says the colours are fine
"They can't hurt you,
it's just in your head!"

"But my head is the thing that's hurting!"

And we go round and round again...

Everywhere I look,
they invade. Every thought,
every glance, every moment.
Even my own reflection is no oasis.

Piercing blonde hair spills
around a pale peach face,
blues eyes subdued while
lips too red snarl in fear.

Blue eyes shut to give way to darkness.
The blackness is beautiful, comforting,
why can't it always be like this?
Why. Can't. It?

Suddenly the reflection cracks,
fiery red trickles down my knuckles

The laughter bubbles up.
The Colours have already won.
They are within me and they are without.
There is no escape,
        so why fight it?
Time can be much better spent on me.
Show them up,
prove I am stronger,
make them regret questioning me.

Blues eyes flicker open,
this time burning bright with spite

Colourful Questions

How would you define a colour?
With emotion?
Primarily speaking--
Would blue be the calm contentedness of a day
well spent?
Could red be the fiery passion that gets our
blood pumping?
Maybe yellow is simply the unbridled joy that
launches us skyward?
But then--
What of the secondary colours?
Or the complex emotions?
Is orange suppressed rage?
And what hellish emotional range gives rise to..
beige?
And further, who am I to dictate how you feel
your emotions?
Who am I to assert such labels?

How then, do we define colour?
Can we relate it to animals?
Seasons?
Furniture??!

Maybe, just maybe,

They are what they are
It is what it is
And the quest of life is to accept that.

What is an ending?

Many people are saddened
when things end
It seems that everything must come to a
        stop.
But really, it is just the close of a book,
the shutting of a door,
the final downing of an eyelid before sleep.
We do not know what the future holds,
but we can enjoy the moment we are
        in.
An ending doesn't have to mean it's over,
it's just a save point for memories.
Wonderful memories, cherished memories,
sad memories, painful...
These all shape us to who we are in the present
So can it ever be truly over?
So I reject an end and simply say
        until next time!